UNDERSTAND YOUR

Mind AND Body

Obesity

Kit Caudron-Robinson

Explore other books at:
WWW.ENGAGEBOOKS.COM

VANCOUVER, B.C.

e WWW.ENGAGEBOOKS.COM

Obesity: Understand Your Mind and Body
Kit Caudron-Robinson 1996 –
Text © 2023 Engage Books
Design © 2023 Engage Books

Edited by: A.R. Roumanis Ashley Lee,
Melody Sun, and Sarah Harvey
Design by: Mandy Christiansen

Text set in Montserrat Regular.
Chapter headings set in Hobgoblin.

FIRST EDITION / FIRST PRINTING

LIBRARY AND ARCHIVES CANADA CATALOGUING IN PUBLICATION

Title: Obesity: Understand Your Mind and Body Level 3 reader / K Caudron-Robinson
Names: Kit Caudron-Robinson 1996- author

Identifiers: Canadiana (print) 20200308874 | Canadiana (ebook) 20200308912
ISBN 978-1-77476-974-4 (hardcover)
ISBN 978-1-77476-975-1 (softcover)
ISBN 978-1-77476-977-5 (pdf)
ISBN 978-1-77476-976-8 (epub)
ISBN 978-1-77878-113-1 (audio)

Subjects:
LCSH: Obesity—Juvenile literature.
LCSH: Obesity in children—Juvenile literature.

Classification: LCC BF723.A4 J66 2023 | DDC J152.4/7—DC23

This project has been made possible in part
by the Government of Canada.

Canadá

Contents

What Is Obesity?

Obesity is a **chronic** medical condition. It happens when someone has more fat on their body than what is healthy. Everyone has some fat on their body, but too much can cause health problems.

KEY WORD

Chronic: something that lasts for a long time.

Obesity causes over 4 million deaths each year around the world.

Some people only have a little extra fat on their bodies. This is called being overweight. Obesity means a person has a lot of extra fat on their body.

A doctor will do tests to figure out if someone has extra fat on their body.

What Causes Obesity?

Obesity can be **genetic**. Children with obese parents are more likely to develop obesity. Some diseases and medicines can also cause obesity.

KEY WORD

Genetic: traits that are passed down from one family member to another.

Not getting enough exercise or healthy food can also lead to obesity. Some people may find it hard to do outdoor exercises because they do not have enough green space nearby. Some people cannot find healthy food where they live, or they do not have enough money to buy it.

Food deserts are places in cities where it is hard to find fresh food.

How Does Obesity Affect Your Brain?

The **prefrontal cortex** is the part of the brain used for memory, decision making, and controlling thoughts and emotions. Sometimes obesity can make it hard for this area to work normally. People can then have problems thinking, remembering, or planning.

Prefrontal Cortex

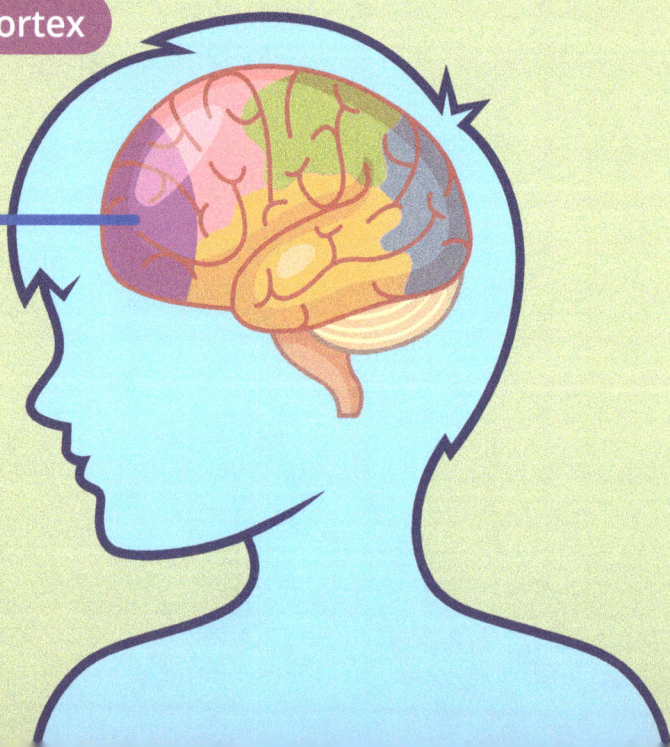

Obesity also affects mental health. It can cause **anxiety**. People may worry they are being judged for their weight.

Anxiety: feelings of worry and fear that are hard to control.

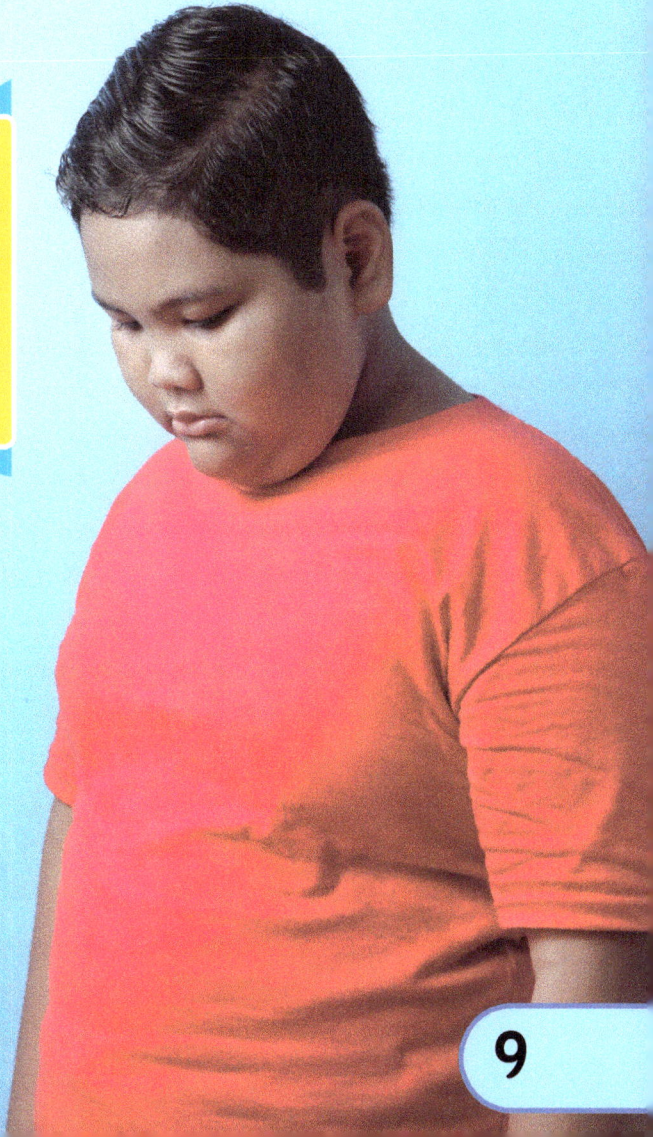

How Does Obesity Affect Your Body?

Extra weight can be hard on people's bones and **joints**. They can become damaged. Obesity can also cause problems with breathing.

KEY WORD

Joints: places in the body where two or more bones meet.

Some people with obesity have trouble sleeping.

Obesity can lead to health problems like heart disease, **diabetes**, and some cancers. Obesity is the number one reason people get diabetes. Getting to a healthy weight can lower the chances of getting these problems.

KEY WORD

Diabetes: a chronic disease that affects how much sugar is in a person's blood.

What Is Weight Bias?

Weight bias means treating people poorly based on stereotypes about obesity. Stereotypes are unfair or untrue beliefs about a person or a group of people. Stereotypes about obesity include the belief that people with obesity are lazy or do not want to change.

Being overweight or obese is the number one reason children are bullied.

Some doctors with a weight bias may not give an obese person the medical care they need. They think all of an obese person's problems are because of their weight. Sometimes they do not believe someone who is overweight or obese can be healthy.

Obese people often avoid seeking medical care because of weight bias.

Can Obesity Go Away?

If obesity is caused by a genetic problem, it may be very difficult to deal with. Very few people lose weight and keep it off. Success should be measured in health, not in weight loss.

Doctors who study obesity prefer to use the term "weight management" rather than "weight loss."

Lifestyle changes can improve well-being for some people with obesity. Eating healthy foods like fruits and vegetables can help give a person energy and keep them healthy. Exercising can do this as well.

KEY WORD

Lifestyle: the way someone lives.

Talk to a doctor if you think you are obese. They can help you understand what is going on in your body.

Asking for Help

Asking for help can be scary, but it is an important step in becoming healthier. A doctor can help support you. Friends and family can **motivate** you.

KEY WORD

Motivate: give someone reasons to work towards a goal.

"I think I might be obese and would like to talk to a doctor about it."

"I would like to eat healthier. Can you help me come up with some healthy foods to eat?"

"I need to be more active. Do you want to be my exercise buddy?"

How to Help Others With Obesity

You cannot fix someone else's obesity. But you can support the changes they are trying to make. Make sure your friend knows they are loved for who they are, not how much they weigh.

Be an exercise buddy
Play sports or go swimming together. Sometimes exercise is more fun with a friend.

Share healthy food

Ask an adult to make sure there are healthy snacks in the house if you have a friend visiting. You could even learn to make a healthy recipe together.

Encourage them

Encouraging someone means making them feel like they can reach their goal. Let your friend know you believe in them. Celebrate with them when they reach small goals.

The History of Obesity

Obesity has been around a very long time. Scientists have found statues of obese women made over 20,000 years ago. The most popular is called the Venus of Willendorf. Some people believe these statues show that obesity was **valued** at that time.

KEY WORD

Valued: thought to be important.

In Ancient Greece and Rome, doctors believed eating smaller amounts could help obesity. They also thought obesity could be helped by going for a walk in the morning and a run at night. Some doctors thought warm baths could help.

Many fake cures for obesity were sold in the 1800s. These included rubber clothes and creams people could rub on their bodies. Some people thought bathing in cold water could cure obesity.

Obesity Superheroes

Some people do not like to talk about their weight. Others do. Here are some obesity superheroes who have opened up about their weight and their health.

John Goodman weighed almost 400 pounds in 2007. The actor was told he was going to have diabetes. He started eating a healthy diet and exercising six days a week. By 2021, he had lost 200 pounds.

Eating healthier amounts of food is a big part of Goodman's diet plan.

Actor **Arjun Kapoor** has been fighting obesity since he was a child. He has lost a lot of weight, and he is working hard to keep healthy. He believes going for walks is one of the best things people can do for their health.

Mo'Nique is an actress and comedian who has struggled with her weight for years. She started exercising and eating differently and feels healthier in her body. She knows her size does not matter, but her health does.

Obesity Tip 1: Eating Healthy

Try to eat plenty of fruits and vegetables. These foods have lots of healthy **nutrients**. Choose whole grains to help you feel full faster so you end up eating less. Brown rice and quinoa are great choices.

KEY WORD

Nutrients: substances in food that help people, animals, and plants live and grow.

Eat lots of **protein**. Chicken, fish, beans, and nuts will help you feel full. Eat small meals throughout the day. This helps keep your energy levels up all day.

KEY WORD

Protein: a substance found in plants and animals that helps keep muscles and other parts of the body healthy.

Try adding lemon or berries to water instead of having sweet drinks.

Obesity Tip 2: Exercising

Choose activities that are fun for you. Start small. It is okay to begin with only a few minutes a day. Weight training helps boost your **metabolism**.

KEY WORD

Metabolism: the way our body turns food into energy.

Keep your workouts interesting. Try something you have not done before. Remember to listen to your body. Take breaks when you need them.

Do not forget to drink lots of water!

Obesity Tip 3: Connecting With Others

Connecting with other people with obesity can be helpful. They can offer their support. Online communities can give you tips and advice.

Find a workout buddy. Having a friend beside you will be a big help. Talk to your doctor about support in your community.

Quiz

Test your knowledge of obesity by answering the following questions. The questions are based on what you have read in this book. The answers are listed on the bottom of the next page.

1 How many deaths are caused by obesity each year?

2 What are food deserts?

3 Does obesity affect mental health?

4 What is the number one reason people get diabetes?

5 What does weight bias mean?

6 What term do doctors who study obesity prefer to use rather than "weight loss"?

Explore Other Level 3 Readers.

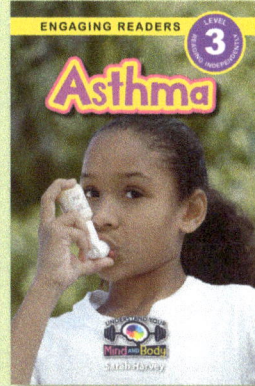

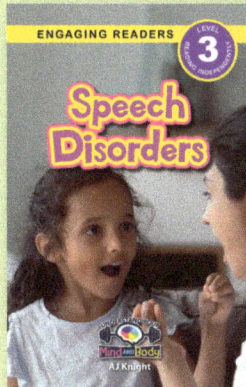

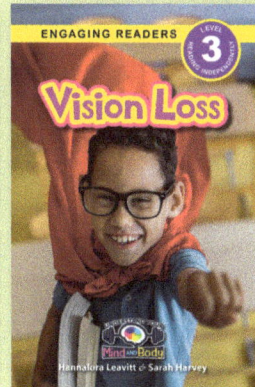

ENGAGING READERS LEVEL 3
ADHD
AJ Knight

ENGAGING READERS LEVEL 3
Anxiety
Adelaide Wilder

ENGAGING READERS LEVEL 3
Asthma
Sarah Harvey

ENGAGING READERS LEVEL 3
Body Image
Adelaide Wilder

ENGAGING READERS LEVEL 3
Dyslexia
Sarah Harvey

ENGAGING READERS LEVEL 3
Diabetes
Kit Caudron-Robinson

ENGAGING READERS LEVEL 3
Obesity
Kit Caudron-Robinson

ENGAGING READERS LEVEL 3
Speech Disorders
AJ Knight

ENGAGING READERS LEVEL 3
Vision Loss
Hannalora Leavitt & Sarah Harvey

Visit www.engagebooks.com/readers

www.ingramcontent.com/pod-product-compliance
Lightning Source LLC
Chambersburg PA
CBHW051238020426
42331CB00016B/3437